Farm to Table

Keep On Truckin'
Volume V - Changing Thrones

ROCK

Farm To Table

Keep On Truckin'

Volume V – Changing Thrones

Copyright © 2023

by ROCK

All rights reserved. No portion of this book may be reproduced, stored in a retrieval system, or transmitted in any form or by any means electronic, mechanical, photocopy, recording, scanning, or other—except for brief quotations in reviews or articles, without the prior written permission of the author.

Printed in the United States of America by Kindle Direct Publishing

Some names and identifying details have been changed to protect the privacy of individuals. Readers should be aware that Internet Web sites offered as citations and/or sources for further information may have changed or disappeared between the time this was written and when it is read.

All scripture quotations, unless otherwise indicated, are taken from the Holy Bible, New International Version®, NIV®. Copyright ©1973, 1978, 1984, 2011by Biblica, Inc.™ Used by permission of Zondervan. All rights reserved worldwide. www.zondervan.com The "NIV" and "New International Version" are trademarks registered in the United States Patent and Trademark Office by Biblica, Inc.™

Dedicated to my brother
Terry "Ticky" Shunk
7.19.59-8.2.22
I'll miss you, bro
♡, Rock

Foreword

When someone thinks of a throne they picture someone in a chair giving orders or commands. Notice what is happening during this time? Someone is sitting in a chair resting, someone is usually telling someone else what to do. As I'm thinking of doing something in this life, this verse comes to mind: "Then Jesus told his disciples, if anyone would come after me, let him deny himself and take up his cross and follow me."

Matthew 16:24

To take up his cross means to remove ourselves from the throne, stop sitting and kneel, to pick up the cross of Jesus! After moving ourselves from our throne we had created we realize that the cross has two important features. Since Christ defeated the cross He has proved He is strong enough to forgive us our sins and provide total liberation from it. This liberation allows us to have freedom to do the job Christ has set before us. This newfound freedom also gives us the strength through Christ to follow Him. Following Him will not be an easy road. If sitting on our own earthly throne we try to do this or relying on our own wisdom, we will fail. However, Jesus says in Matthew 11:28 through 30, "Come to me, all you who are weary and burdened, and I will give you rest. Take my yoke upon you and learn from me, for I am gentle and humble in heart, and you will find rest for your souls. For my yoke is easy and my burden is light." Rock's book will talk about changing thrones. She will describe how she was able to go from a desperate girl in the streets of Las Vegas to a mighty woman of God. She did this because she did what Christ asked her to do. Taking herself off the throne and putting Christ in her former place, she not only had a change of thrones but ultimately a change of heart.

I am honored that I was asked to foreword this book. It is a wonderful thing to do, however, nothing compares to the love we share together with Jesus as our Lord and Savior. At the end of this book, you will learn how to have Christ in your heart. You'll experience the joy that Rock and I share. I hope you read the book, but more importantly, I hope you ask Christ to come into your life. If you have not done this, do it now. Change your throne from yourself to one that follows Christ! Do it today!

>Lovingly,
>
>Craig Parker
>
>Pastor, Unity on a Mission. Romans 10:13 "…for everyone who calls on the name of the Lord will be saved. "

Introduction:

Everything new. Glory to God, everything's new. And so, I left you on *Heartbreak Mountain* when everything became new after the demon fled the Ponderosa and so we are going to get back into the series. I'm going to kind of go back and forth so that you guys can get caught up and remember some of the things that happened throughout the volumes. So, as we are going through these different chapters, as I'm explaining the things that happened, I am giving as much glory as I can to the Almighty God who created every single one of us. I want to go ahead and insert a lot of things that I've missed, since it has been brought to my attention. I need to go ahead and make that happen for y'all, so that you get the whole jest of the story.

Because it is quite a story, and it needs to be told and so everything's new. I named this book *Changing Thrones* because everything became new when I basically "changed thrones". Now what does that mean? That means that the throne that I thought that I was serving was basically Satan's throne, and now we're writing in book #5 or Volume 5, the Throne of the Almighty God. His name is Elohim. His name is Yahweh. He's has many names. So, we are serving Him now which is quite a difference.

When He makes everything new, He's not even kidding! Things that are new are not just material things. That means that, He made Me new, He made my daughter Samantha new. He made everything new even though it looked like there was a lot of death. And there was. There were a lot of things that had to die, so that some newness could come. If y'all have lived on the planet long enough, you know that a lot of times you will see death, and then you will see some babies born. Then you'll see some tragedy, but then you will get to see some beauty out of it. Beauty will come out of it.

Farm to Table – Volume V

If you will watch it, you'll get to see God moving in His miraculous ways that only He can do, and we can give Him all the Glory. So that is my opening statement basically for He makes everything new!

Now, I'm going to get into the volumes. Here I go. I have had quite a bit of things happen since I wrote to you last. I can't wait until we get to Volumes 16-19! That would be the time frame that I'm basically speaking about now and it really ramps up and it's very good stuff. Hold on for y'all are in for quite a ride. So, remember what I always tell ya, "Keep on trucking, Peace be with you". Keep on reading! It's only going to get better and better, alright? Peace!

Chapter One

I Must Decrease so that He can Increase.

I must decrease means that I need to get away from thinking that I'm doing all of this and recognize that it is God that is doing all of this. So, at this time everything's all cleaned up. It looks good. The place doesn't have that creepy stalker vibe anymore at The Ponderosa, but now it's time we get to work. We weren't sure exactly what to do.

I had a girl that worked for me before whose name was Heidi. I had taught her how to be a dispatcher. She ended up going over to Jefferson, Georgia and finding this guy named Zond, and she talked him into opening her up a brokerage. Well, she got him started because he had tons of money, but she really didn't know what she was doing. She knew how to dispatch, she just didn't understand business.

I got a call from her one day and she said "Hey Rock, can you please come to the office over here in Jefferson, and talk to me?" At that time, I had no clue that she was dispatching over there. I just went over there to see her. I went in this old creepy building that Zond was operating out of. Zond was a realty guy, and he had taken her on to make money and he didn't know anything about

ROCK

the trucking industry and neither did she, but she did get it going. God Bless her soul.

The day I went in there, she was in there by herself. Zond wasn't there that day. There she was in the back room of this old cotton mill (I think it was). She was back there booking trucks and didn't have a clue what she was really doing. She could load the trucks and get them delivered, but she didn't understand the rest of the business. Zond was a businessman, so he understood that once a truck delivered, it would have to have a bill and a bill of lading. He knew that much and so he started billing.

Farm to Table – Volume V

As the business was going, I guess they were probably about 6 months in, when she started to panic because she had some COD checks in Laredo, Texas (on the Mexican border) that didn't get picked up. This caused them to start to lose money. Heidi was afraid of Zond and she didn't really know what to do. I went in there and looked at the place and said "Heidi, what are you doing?" and she said "I'm just trying to make a living, Rock, but I don't know what I'm doing. I'm scared to tell him that I don't know what I'm doing. Can't you please help me? Can't you just do something? Please help me!"

ROCK

I started looking at her desk and I started looking around. I saw paperwork everywhere. I saw stuff that she had crammed in the back of her desk. I was just mortified for him. I had a heart for this guy that I didn't know and hadn't even met yet. I just knew that the based on job that she was doing, if I didn't try to help them, then he was really going to lose a lot of money. So, I said "Listen, I'll come talk to you later." She said, "Please, I'll make an appointment for you to talk to him… can't you just please come talk to him?" So, I agreed to the appointment.

The day comes for the appointment. She had set me an appointment for that following Wednesday or something. So, I came in and I sat down, and you could tell that he was a businessman and he was used to talking to people. He and I just started chit-chatting and I tell him a little bit about me and I ask him about Heidi and how well did he know her and this and that. Heidi had told him enough about me that he had kind of had an idea that I was an old warhorse of trucking.

He had very many questions. He started asking me all kinds of questions. Like, was I working? And what was I doing? And of course at that time, I wasn't working because I had shut the company down if you remember correctly in *Heartbreak Mountain*

ROCK

because my granddaughter had died of the Leukemia. So, I was basically out of work.

He asked me if I wanted to work there. I told him if I was going to work for him then, "I had to have my team. It's just not me and when I come to you, I'm coming to you with my team or I'm not coming to you at all." Because we were just that: a team. He said "really?' and I said, "Yeah". If you remember correctly, Sammy (after Tabitha died) took a ride to Florida. She was down there for quite some time just trying to get herself together. She would be part of the team.

There were a total of 5 girls that I would need to call. I told Zond that I would have to call all the girls and see if they were interested in working. Reminding him that he would end up having to buy a team. He agreed with me and he really couldn't believe it. He couldn't believe it was a real "team". He couldn't believe that they actually existed. I told him that I'd get back with him and that I'd make another appointment.

I sat down and I wrote a proposal. This proposal outlined the amount of dollars for the team and other requirements for us to start. First, we would have to gut the office. We would have to have new phones and we

ROCK

would have to have this and that. If he accepted the proposal we would get on it.

I started calling the girls (one by one) to see what they were doing. One of their names was Judo, her real name was Judy. I called her and said, "what are you doing, Judo?" We always called each other "bitty" which is a nice way of saying something else, so she said, "I'm not doing anything bitty, what do you have in mind?" Then I called the next one, she said "no, I'm not doing anything, what do you have in mind?" By the time I got to Sammy (I finally found Sammy) I told her "Well I'm going to make an appointment for us to go sit down with this guy named Zond, and let's talk to him. If everybody agrees that we are going to work, then we are going to go in there and clean up Heidi's mess. We will need to figure out what she has done and what she didn't do. We'll try to make some sense out of it, so we can get the brokerage turned back around for him."

Chapter 2

Making the Deal with Zond

We had a new appointment to speak with Zond about the proposal. The girls and I went to the appointment one evening. We met with him and his wife (who was a very nice lady). We had the proposal drawn up. We sat down and talked with him and everybody kind of introduced themselves. He and his wife were just absolutely blown away that we were all in one accord. Basically, we were in unity. A unified team. We really were. The fact that all of us were out of work at the same time was a miracle from God anyway and I couldn't believe it. Even when I was making the phone calls to them, I couldn't believe every single one of them was out of work because everyone one of them were professionals.

It was just a God timing thing. We are at this meeting and he's going around the table; they're talking to each one of the girls, asking them different questions, this and that. Every one of them were in agreement. They were like "Ok!" So, I told him, "If y'all are willing to sign this proposal, we will give you a two-year window." It was a two year mission.

ROCK

The name of the company was Zonco. For all of you readers out there, you may or may not have had a good experience with them. God bless your souls.

Mr. Zond was a real estate tycoon. He had invested into a business that he was unfamiliar with because it was quite a different business (even though most businesses are the same), so he needed our expertise.

In the meantime, my daughter Jody (who had her son Ty who was about 5, the same age as Tabitha was) she had her own little business doing her own little thing. She had tried out being a broker on her own and so she was working her own little agency. She wasn't part of this particular team at Zonco. She would end up part of the team before it was over.

We got started and the first thing that we did was gut the place. We needed time to gut the place, to get it set up and see what Heidi had crammed in the back of her drawers. We had to get organized and particularly get a filing system going. I mean it was absolutely a… ya know, it was kind of like you've seen these shows that you watch on TV, like fix that old house in some bazaar way. We went in there and we worked hard.

ROCK

I noticed that Zond would always watch Sammy a lot. He was mostly interested in Sammy. At some point, I think he called her the "Golden Goose" (which made me real mad, I got pissed). I'm just willingly being honest with you, I just don't like that. She was very good at her job, but you couldn't single one of them out because it took the whole team. It really did. Actually, it takes a village to do anything. I had learned that when I went to the bible school I was telling you about back in *Heartbreak Mountain*. When I started going to those classes and learned that God is all about unity. I had created unity with the girls and didn't even realize that was what I was doing. That was just my personality and who I was and actually how I was trained up throughout the years.

The girls got the office looking like a "jewel", so we started working. The phones were ringing and Zond was really happy. One of the drivers came in one day and as he was washing his hands in the sink, he looks over at me and he said "you know what you remind me of?' I said "What?" he said, "you remind me of ants." In the Word of God (the Bible) it says to look at the ants you sluggard. Which means: follow the ants' ways. They don't have any leader, yet they still produce, and they still work, and they keep going and they keep going. So, we were kind of like the ants he said. I thought that was a good analogy because that is the truth.

We would work from 8 o'clock in the morning to sometimes 8 o'clock at night. We always made sure all the drivers were taken care of. We would make sure all things were happening and we never left any of our drivers out in the cold. We always took the phone with us and to this day we still take the phones with us. That way if a driver had a problem, he could always get somebody on the phone. Even now currently, most businesses don't do that (even brokerages) they just leave you hanging. Once they are closed, they're closed. That's just not good business in the trucking industry because the truckers are the backbone of the country. For that reason, we take care of our guys and they take care of us (we learned that).

The team is going along, and we are doing a really good job (I think). I personally think Zond is impressed. He was teaching me some accounting techniques that I didn't know, and I enjoyed that. I really fought it at first, but I really embraced it after a while. He was bound and determined (I think he was like 15 years older than me) he wanted to teach me some stuff. We're supposed to keep a teachable spirit, and I had a teachable spirit even though I tended to buck him and be somewhat stubborn. I still did what he was showing me to do because he was good

ROCK

at it. He taught me a lot about the computer, he taught me things that I needed to know.

During that time, I used a stage name. Many times we used a different name than our actual legal name. I used a stage name and I would always tell everybody, "I am Kit Parson's on the job". They would laugh. I was in charge of the payables and also the receivables. I did the accounting with girl named Gloria, I called her my Mexican. She helped me in every aspect of accounting. Accounting in trucking is very hard and it's very tedious work.

We always worked pretty hard. Then all of a sudden, (we were about a year and a half in) Zond and his wife decided that they wanted to sell the brokerage to me and my daughter Sammy. That right there was quite a blow. I was almost up on my two years. It was coming around. It was probably a couple months out and Zond comes up with this idea of how we should buy the business from him.

Chapter 3

Two years is up. Buy the business.

Zond comes with a proposal for us. Now if you remember correctly in *Heartbreak Mountain,* in the last chapter was where the demon flees, Jed, he went to Ohio, but that didn't mean he left me alone. In the two years that we were at Zonco, I had literally taken a beaten from Jed over the telephone. That meant that he called every single day and he basically tortured me and the girls verbally. The girls all knew him, and so they didn't really take him seriously, but I was still married to him. Since I was still married to him, I thought that I was supposed to have to listen to all his stuff. I was just living through it knowing God would provide a way, a hiding place for me no matter what I was going through.

Even though I was the female (contrary to most marriages) I had to play the male role. Many men typically have to pay their wives (exes) alimony but in my case, I was paying Jed! He was supposed to be the bread winner in the family (yeah right). So, every week, for 2 years, I would send him $500 via FedEx. Believe it or not, that would never shut him up. That's a lot of money ($500 a week for 2 years)!! I'm mentioning this part

ROCK

because it will play into Zond's rate of making a deal.

We were interested in buying the business and all of that, but I still had Jed out there yapping and I still wasn't divorced yet. And so, the divorce had to happen. It had to get done, so that I could carry on as a Christian soldier and do my thing. So, I literally, I don't even know how it happened, I can't even remember exactly how the divorce happened, but it did. I finally got Judo (one of the dispatchers) who told me to how get a TPO (which I didn't even know what that was). If you don't know is a temporary protection order from the judge. This meant he had to stay away from me and not contact me. I think that just escalated the divorce, and finally the paperwork was signed, and it was a done deal! I was able to change my name back to my maiden name and was finally out of the marriage.

Well, in the meantime, the 2 years is almost up, and Zond is over there, he wants me and Sammy to buy the business. Now he didn't want hard cash, he wanted the receivables. Which if you don't know is money on paper, basically. Zond wanted the receivables which would mean we would have to start from scratch with no money and climb our way back up the pile, which was ridiculous! We didn't really want to do that, so we created a deal with him where we

ROCK

would all be satisfied and everybody would gain in this.

The plan was we would keep the name and he would be able to bow out. They were getting older and they didn't want the pressure of the brokerage and all it entails. We had a little table (a closing table) in the board room. When we met in there, Zond was trying to tie the deal to my property (my personal real estate, The Ponderosa)! Sammy jumped up in that meeting and said, "Hell No! You're not getting my mom's land". His wife, didn't even know that was in the contract, so she said "Take it easy, just scratch that part out and just do the deal anyway with this and that". So, I'm like

"Help me! Are you sure we are supposed to do this deal?" At that time, Sammy and I weren't positive we were supposed to do the deal. We were kind of like back up off us and let us try to decide whether or not we are in God's timing or not.

In the meantime, my daughter Jody, she had been going down her own dusty trail with her company, so she decided to come work with us at Zonco. She was helping in dispatch (she can do any part of the business) so, she was an asset to us. She came in and I told her that I wasn't sure how it was going to go with Zond. That he was trying to get us to buy the business and maybe she should look for us another avenue. Maybe we could be an agent for somebody.

So, I was driving around just thinking one day and saw Landstar opening up a terminal Jefferson. It was somewhere on the outskirts of the highway. I came back in the office, and I told Jody, why don't you get Landstar on the line and let's get somebody in here and let me talk to them. And so, Jody did that. That's when I met Wade (to this day he is one of my best friends). Wade came in and at that time he was the regional manager for Landstar. He came into the office and he saw the brokerage in action. He couldn't deny that we knew how to do the job. So, we basically signed up with

Landstar as an agency and Wade was our regional guy.

That move gave us a fail-safe because Zonco was a little shaky. We weren't sure what was going to happen with Zond and with him trying to force us to buy the business, we weren't sure if that was going to work. I had a conversation with Zond and I told him that we needed to move the girls out of the cotton mill to higher ground. This meant that we needed to get out there, our two years was up, and we really needed to get out of there. I told him that Sammy and I would buy the business, but we needed to take it to higher ground to get to a different environment. He said, "No" and I said, "Oh

ROCK

no, don't say no". This was after we had signed the paperwork. So I was thinking: He really can't say no because we own the business, if we go, the business goes. I knew we had to get out of there because it was kind of like a hole in the wall.

We ended up opening a Landstar office on the main drag in Jefferson. This was mainly to prepare ourselves for anything that might happen because Zond wasn't being realistic because he didn't have any more skin in the game. Since he didn't have any skin in the game and he was just wanting to make sure his money was there, he didn't feel the same way as he did when he owned the company.

Farm to Table – Volume V

So, I walked into to talk to the girls and I said, "Has anybody ever left your husband?" and they were all like "Yes!" And I said "well we are going to have to leave, ok, so y'all don't book any more loads. We are just going to go". We can't carry Zond, Jed with his whacking, all this other stuff, and operate and not go off the deep end. So literally we basically said, "We're leaving!"

Chapter 4
Build the Library

We ended up going to the building across the street that was around the corner from Zond's office. We basically moved everything out of the office. We left the phone system. We left the computers. We left everything that he had bought. We didn't take any of it. We just left. We basically shut the business down and left Zonco.

He had taken several thousand dollars and we couldn't really operate. We were just mortified, but we knew that if we went with Landstar that we would recover. The beauty of being an agent was they paid the trucks, they paid the people, and we didn't have to worry about the accounting. Actually, we didn't have to worry about anything.

About that time, I had the Holy Ghost tell me that He wanted me to build a library: a Christian Library. I said, "Lord, I don't even know how to build a library?" I never even liked the library whenever I went to school. He said, "Build the library". So, I called my Pastor Mark (who was also my teacher) and I shared with him that God wanted me to build a library. He said, "do it". I was like Ok, I'll do it.

ROCK

I started building the library in the back of Landstar office in Jefferson. We started by planning the layout. We had to build some shelves, gather the books, materials, everything. While I'm back there building the library, we are still trying to get away from the Jed and Zonco and all of that nightmare and start new. Doing the library was crazy because it was something I never pictured myself doing at all, but I knew God wanted me to do it. I had these guys come in and build these shelves and I told the carpenters to make these shelves where they can be removed because we were renting the office there in Jefferson.

Farm to Table – Volume V

So, I'm building the library, Jody was playing a key role in the start up with Landstar, Sammy was over there shutting down Zonco and it was hard work. The truckers, they were getting mad because we were shutting down the business and I don't hardly blame them. One of the truckers that we used a lot, I won't really name him in this book (but it goes along with an animal), he comes into the Landstar office asking for me. Jody was running the front and I was in the back of the building in the Christian library. She comes back there and says "Look, there is this guy out here who wants to talk to you" I said, "Ok! Send him in here". He comes in the back and says "What are you doing"? I say, "I'm building a Christian library". And he said, "Really? Well ya know, Zonco owes me a lot of money!" I said, "I do know this, but I can't get it. I can't really get it for you because I'm not in charge of it anymore". Basically, Zond had the money. Then I proceeded to tell him the story of what happened.

You know, there still are nice people on the planet y'all. So, we had the talk, me and this guy, it was quite a sum of money and he literally forgave me for the money and he said "You just keep on building for the Lord! I can take this hit". And then he left. It was just one of God's many miracles. I was so thankful. I don't know how else to say it.

Farm to Table – Volume V

Don't think that God doesn't know every single thing that is going to happen with you, to you, and through you. He has a plan for it all. It just blew everybody's mind when I told them that this man was so forgiving. And he was. The truth shall set you free. I just told him the story. I told him what happened. How we ended up at Zonco. How we went through the death. How we cleaned up the place. I told them about the fires. I told him the whole nine. He was just a generally nice man. He forgave the debt. So, we carried on.

Now here comes the attack. The truckers were coming into Jefferson, and they were looking everywhere for us. We didn't know exactly what to do. The truckers, they were looking for their money. So finally, I sent them to Zond and he started paying them and that was good because we couldn't. He had the money. We didn't have the money to do it. We only had what we were making with Landstar which wasn't a lot because we had just started with them.

We got through that attack of everybody that was just mad because we had closed down Zonco. I mean they were just mad. Zonco literally could have survived if the man would have listened and would have let me do what I needed to do for the survival of the company, but that's another story, that's a long story. That would be a business 101 thing that I'd probably have to tell you about later. I did want you to know that while we are fleeing from Zonco, it seemed like we were fleeing from this, that and everything else.

We made some good and some bad decisions, just like everybody does. At the same time, I thought we were trying to make good decisions. The Christian library was one of the better decisions because it lives on to this day, but I've got to tell ya what happened to it, because it was absolutely just amazing. It was amazing how God dealt with it. And so, in the next chapter, I'm going to tell you what happened with the library.

Chapter 5

Mold Attacks Library

I'm getting the library built. I'm ordering the supplies for the library; books, Bibles, CD's, DVD's, all sorts of different materials. As I'm ordering them I asked the Lord, I said "Lord, I need somebody to help me with this library because I really don't know how to build a library." So, he sent me a girl named Ruth. Ruth did the utility locating for the underground city works. She was a very mentally organized lady. She was a red head. She did the basic organization of the library. She literally put it into the computer, organized it and it got it to looking like it was a real library. I was noticing that people were donating different materials and stuff for the library. I noticed that all of a sudden that there was this smell of mold. Now you guys know what the smell of mold is when you smell it. The moldy smell was a dusty mold. Well all of a sudden there was this mold attack. The fungus or whatever it was started moving to our other books and other supplies and it started to take over the library.

Well, I went to the Lord with it. I really did. I went to the Lord, and I said "What do I do about this? You said build the library" and He said, "Look at Leviticus". So I went to Leviticus in the Bible and literally the

ROCK

whole story about mold was in there. Red mold, black mold, and green mold and what the priest did back in the day when somebody would show up with this mold, it was the most interesting thing. I couldn't even believe it. I couldn't believe that it was in the Bible. It was so interesting that I thought it was just crazy. You just know it was the Lord teaching me something. So, he showed me that it was an attack. So, I told the Landlord, I said, "you need to do something about this mold in this building, because it's getting on our goods". They said they would do something, they would send somebody to do some bleaching and this and that. Well, nothing worked.

Farm to Table – Volume V

So finally, we didn't have enough money to make the rent. The rent was outrageous there anyway. However, we knew we had to leave regardless because of our health. God always provides a way of escape, y'all. So, I'm like I don't' know what we are going to do. I said "Jody, I don't know what we are going to do" I told Sammy the same thing, but we've got to move this library and we've got to move ourselves somewhere.

Chapter 6

Moving Back

We decided to move back to the Ponderosa, to the basement of the house. I wrote a letter to the rental people and told them that we were evacuating the building due to the mold, and we were out of there. I called the guys up that built the shelves and told them to get over there. The dudes came out there to move the shelves from the library and move them to the Ponderosa, and do you know that those shelves fit exactly on the walls in the basement of the Ponderosa! It freaked the carpenters out so bad! When they put the shelves on the walls, the measurements were exact and I couldn't have possibly known the measurements on the walls, but God knew. It freaked them out so bad that they put the shelves up then they were just chomping at the bit to get their check and then they were like "Give me the check, you're freaking us out" and they ran for their lives. They put the shelves up and ran for their lives! Then we brought the library materials to the Ponderosa since the shelves were in.

So, we just started building it from there. It was crazy. But the thing was, it was just like God told Noah when he gave the exact dimensions of the Ark, He was not kidding.

ROCK

He gave him exact instructions of how to build the ark and really, he did the same with me with this library. It seemed like it was nuts building the library, but the only one who didn't think I was nuts was Mark, which was my pastor, teacher, mentor, and he knew I wasn't nuts and he knew that I was listening. He knew I was just trying to do what I was here on the planet to do.

So, the library ends up in the basement and so did Landstar. It ended up in the basement of the Ponderosa. We moved our phones, our library, the whole nine yards, and put it in the Ponderosa basement so we wouldn't go out of business. We would now have a way to make money and carry on our

Christian soldiers. We get all settled in at the Ponderosa with the library and the business and the next thing I know I get a phone call from Pastor Mark, he says "I need an appointment with you" and I tell him, "Ok well, Come on over. I got an appointment. Come on in".

He comes over and it wasn't like him to just show up really fast, like out of the blue or even to make an appointment for that matter, but he was there. Doing what he was supposed to. Praying when he was supposed to. He showed up and I'll never forget what he was wearing. He had a Krispy Kreme hat on, and he was sitting in the corner of my office, and I was smoking. So, there was

ROCK

smoke in the room and he is sitting in the corner and he says "I got to tell you something, Rock. This lady comes up to me at church and says that the Lord told her to give him $5000 for a library. And so, he says, "I guess that is your cue, Rock. Move the library to the church. I'll get the shelves built and move it to the church". To me that was just confirmation that I was on the right track. I mean I couldn't believe it. He couldn't believe it. Well, he could believe it. Ya know, we just both went with it.

Chapter 7
Hummingbird Confirmation

As the library was being transitioned I'm sitting upstairs at my table, because it's *Farm to Table*, so I'm sitting at the table, a hummingbird keeps coming up to my window. He keeps looking at me and fluttering. So, I see this little hummingbird and I was talking to it. You know "How ya doing little hummingbird?" And it would fly away. I didn't think much about it at the time, until we had the opening for the library. Mark had the shelves in the library already at the church. We had such good material that the people would just come in all the time and check the stuff out and then bring it back. The library was in the church for I guess a couple of years. We really never promoted the library, but we did have a grand opening.

The lady that gave the $5000 to Mark for the library was the wife of one of Mark's professors at UGA where he went to school, and before he died, he told his wife that he wanted Mark to have a library. That is how the library came about.

The day of the grand opening, the lady showed up and she brought a plan and everything. She had on this pin, and it was a

ROCK

pin of a hummingbird. I mentioned the hummingbird that was on her shirt, and she told me that her husband was all about hummingbirds. And I thought that was crazy good, that the hummingbird kept coming to the window there and talking to me during this time of building the library. She had listened to her husband, listened to the Lord. A lot of people got to feed off that library.

I'll tell you more about it later in the series'. But you know, let's say, 20 years later, the library still exists and was destined to go to the prisons, to the wayward souls in the prison and to this day, it's operating in the prisons especially in Florida. It's really good work for Jesus. He has a plan and a reason for everything He puts you through and anything He wants you to do for Him. It is a tool for the Master's use. I had to be obedient to the Lord in order to get this library to touch the people that it's touching.

I just want to let you know that if you have a mission from God, no matter how crazy it might look, it is God Himself who is moving you towards that direction. Just like the prisons and the library. Who knew through all of that, that He had a plan to make sure that the prisoners would get a Bible or a book with the Word. There's something about the books that we are sending out, *Armed and Dangerous*, they are awesome. They break down different things like fear, anxiety, depression, things that the prisoners are going through. What we are all are going through actually. They break it down for the prisoners to help them to be able to cope. To give them some coping mechanisms while they are in there trying to re-habilitate themselves. It's a really good work and just know that if God puts you to it, He will get you through it.

Chapter 8

Frani "Fang" Returns

We became Landstar at the Ponderosa in the basement. Most of the girls went and did something different after Zonco. The ones that were left were: Becky, Mexican and Kathy. We all were in the basement working for Landstar. Jody started her own little business somewhere in Hoschton. Sammy went to Florida and started a little business down there for a short period. Everybody kind of got split up and did their own thing for a little while.

Farm to Table – Volume V

My sister, Frani, who I hadn't seen for like 15 years, all of a sudden, she comes out of nowhere. Sammy and I used to go this little bar and grill (we didn't drink) we just went there to eat dinner at night. It's a place called Jeffery's. We were sitting there one evening, and my niece Kelli comes in and she is there to visit and Jody shows up at the table too and we are all talking. I ask Kelli, "Where is my sister at?" (Kelli's her daughter) and she didn't say anything. Then I said, "What color is her hair?" The reason I asked this question was because my sister if she died her hair blonde (she was a dark headed, dark-skinned woman) but if she died her hair blonde, then that was an indicator

ROCK

that she was "all over the place". Kelli said, "Her hair is blonde" and I said "Oh no!

Frani, whose nickname was "Fang", I told you about her in one of the earlier volumes. Remember she's from Vegas, so here she walks into the bar and has the blonde hair and I think to myself, "Uh Oh, here we go!" It was definitely on. Here comes my sister after 15 years. I got up, hugged her neck and I said come on let's take a ride out of here, because the bar was so loud, we couldn't really hear each other.

I took her over to the Ponderosa and as we pulled up and the gate opened, she said, "You live here?" And I said, "Yes". She said that she thought that I lived in Acworth, in a trailer, with some cats. The internet was just getting started at this time, she had found my name and went to this trailer with these cats and left a note on the person's door. The note read, "Trick or Treat" signed, Fang. Well the people that got that note were probably wondering who it was from. She didn't realize that I wouldn't have lived in a trailer with cats that just wasn't me.

I took her into the Ponderosa, and she was amazed. She really was. She was in there on her little cell phone calling Nick (her husband) telling him what she had seen and what was going on and this and that.

ROCK

Here comes a new season and just so you guys all know out there, everything has its seasons. Even the Bible says there is a season for everything and everything in its time. And I knew that this season was going to change when I saw her. I was like OK, Jed was out, and here she came, Frani, was in. We were in for a ride in this new season.

I told y'all many times in the previous volumes that He always puts me on a two-year mission. And so, it was always a two-year mission. And I know from experience with Frani comes all kinds of different kinds of something. I hadn't seen her in so many years and there was so much catching up to do, at first I was distracted, but we needed the time together. The girls were in the basement at Landstar, and we weren't really making any money. Jody who was making tons of money at her business, she was coming in and giving me and Becky money to survive. She had such respect for us because we were working so hard just to pay the bills instead of working to get money for ourselves. Jody came in and said, "I got such respect for y'all that I'm just going to give you this money". Becky and I knew that it would take time to build the thing that. We would have to basically take a hit until we got the money to be able to pay ourselves. My sister coming in just about that time too, made it very interesting timing. There is a

ROCK

long long story that goes along with the subject of timing, but I think that is for whole different volume.

My sister Frani moved to Georgia from Las Vegas soon after visiting. As you know Las Vegas and Georgia are about two way different things. When Fang entered the picture Landstar was still in the game. Only God knew that I wanted to have my girls to be seen by somebody on the planet that was a "big dog" like a big company and have them recognized. They were always working in a small hole in the wall somewhere and nobody ever really recognized them except the people on the phones, but they never really saw them. We had been given a trip to

Orlando by Landstar. It was me, Jody, Sammy, Becky, and Mexican and I think a couple of other girls came with us too. The trip to Orlando was God just blessing us.

I'll never forget, I've got these things hanging around my neck and I ask Becky, "What do you think these things are for?" They were like little flags, and she said, "I don't know but I'll find out". She comes back and she says, "Those are because we got a prize coming, we are rookies of the year!" I was like, "How cool is that?" We ended up getting presented with a trophy from Landstar for "Rookie of the year". We were so far from rookies it was crazy, but it was so exciting to see what God was going to do with this.

They had the band *Foreigner* playing for the agents from all around the country because they were million-dollar agents. They had it on the beach and the scenery was just awesome. I was able to get up on stage with my girls and get a picture with the President of Landstar. I got the picture! You know a picture is worth a thousand words y'all. I finally had something that I could show somebody. Here are my girls. Here is what they look like. They are beautiful. God did a beautiful deal with my girls.

So that was just a big God thing; the fact that *Foreigner* was playing, the fact that they were calling us the "Hollywood girls". It was all good. It was God blessing us for our hard labor and service and just paying attention to His business. Because how many of you know we only perform for an audience of One?

We are going to start #6 with a whole new theme and it's going to be what happens when Fang shows up from Las Vegas. That's how I'm going to end this. Peace be with y'all. Thank y'all for reading. Keep up with me. I'm going to keep writing, OK? Keep on Trucking! God Speed. *Rock out!*

Author's Note

Thank you for checking out this next volume of my story. Please stay tuned for future installments of my personal testimony. I believe you'll be blessed by it as you learn from me what I've learned in life. I still have a lot to tell you, and with God's help, I'll get it out to you soon.

Before you go, let's talk for a moment about salvation.

First off, what does "salvation" actually mean? To me, it starts with the fact that all of us have had encounters in our lives which we cannot explain. In my case, when I was young, I had two voices speaking to me from a very young age. One voice told me good things to do, and if I listened to the other one, I went down a dusty trail. In other words, I went the wrong direction.

Farm to Table – Volume V

As we walk this journey together, you'll see in my story just how many times a "higher power" has intervened for me. I really want you to know who this higher power truly is—His name is Jesus Christ. During my ongoing story, I call Him "God" a lot. Truthfully, it was indeed God. For the times I was living through what you just read, I really didn't understand who Jesus was ... and is. But I do now.

Maybe you don't know Jesus either, and that's okay. I'd like to suggest that you look at your own journey. Have there been things you just couldn't explain? Since there isn't any such thing as a coincidence, then who was it exactly that intervened in your life?

I encourage you to take a moment and think about it.

If you want peace, love, joy, and faith, all you have to do is start with a sincere prayer, an example of which follows ...

ROCK

Jesus,

I confess that I have sinned and fallen short of your glory.

I believe that you suffered and died on the cross for me,

And when you did that,

You paid the full price for the punishment due me, for my sins.

Please forgive me for my sins,

And accept me into your kingdom.

Until right now,

Farm to Table – Volume V

I have only lived for myself.

From now on,

I will only live for you.

Thank you for your incredible sacrifice,

And please also show me

How to help others.

When it is my time,

I look forward to being received

Into your glorious presence.

Please come into my life

Now,

And forever …

Welcome to the family!

Don't stop now, there's work to be done.

Notes

Notes

Notes

Notes

www.ingramcontent.com/pod-product-compliance
Lightning Source LLC
Chambersburg PA
CBHW050250220526
45465CB00002B/622